Fear, Some

Fear, Some

poems

Douglas Kearney

RED HEN PRESS | Los Angeles, California

Fear, Some

Book design by Mark E. Cull

ISBN-10: 1-59709-071-9
ISBN-13: 978-1-59709-071-1
Library of Congress Catalog Card Number: 2006922896

The City of Los Angeles Department of Cultural Affairs,
Los Angeles County Arts Commission
and the National Endowment for the Arts
partially support Red Hen Press.

Published by Red Hen Press
First Edition

For Nicole

Acknowledgments

My deepest thanks to the editors of the following publications and websites in which versions of these poems have appeared:

the CalArts MFA Writing website: "Lovepoem Por De-Familiar"
jubilat: "Discount Ritual In 4 Parts: Bag Of Afro" and "The Poet As Setting"
LA-Lit: "At The Pink Teacup", "Auto", "The Orange Alert" and "Shadowboxer On The Lookout"
Mangrove: "Poem With Some Sand And All At Once—SHAITAN!"
nocturnes: "The Chitlin Circuit"

CONTENTS

SCENE FROM "THE POISONOUS COON"

THE POISONOUS COON
Now, y'all repeat after me.

Ink ruins the snow.

"SLAPS I NEEDED"

SHADOWBOXER ON THE LOOKOUT

they wait for me to turn my back
leave something open   they'll climb in
sooty fingerprints staining   drums

push past my dead bolts   window
bars   chain   raise heavy fists
make my home tremble

* * * *

sunday   a woman screams
loud enough to stun a cab   someone
runs in the street   his voice

a flare undershirt blood
his woman all over his hands
it could have been me   both of them

* * * *

smoke on the corner
shadows on the porch
niggers in the street

* * * *

. . . broke into a million pieces   luck already
bad as it can get   now's no time to stare at
mirrors   they're out there   I better . . .

* * * *

nigger eyes rifle through me like some wallet
war drums batter their radios ribcages
swollen with nicotine tough talk   I cross

the street

for Deshawn, Eric, Dallas, Jerome & Lerone

ALAMEDA STREET

We brown boys
    play
            stick games,
    say
            nicknames
like BIG D, EVIL E;
and conjure Knievel
with jigsawed dirt bikes
and sewer curbs
for asphalt launch pads.
    We all sweat
    to know flight
    for just
    a minute.

We brown boys,
    hair
            all knaps,
    wear
            ballcaps'
broken brims. Broken rims
from hungry slamdunks,
pro-ball pipe dreams
over ice cream man's
"Pop Goes the Weasel."
    We all hunt
    change from cords',
    Bermudas
    and mamas.

We brown boys—
    smack
            talking
    slap
            boxing—
stay bragging and bagging,
drinking summer from hoses

and water bomb barrages.
We throw rocks at garages
making no dents.
  We all just
  trying to leave
  a mark.

TEMPER

Those summers, older brothers twisted

knots into fists; made me
show I could escape. When I snapped

the bonds, ran the block's length,

—face smithed with slaps I needed
for strength, rope-soldered wrists

open, chest fired by smoldering adolesence—

I wanted their skins
to claim mine: forged proof of that heavy craft.

FAMILY ROOM

It's nearly over: the violent film
furies in Grandmother's family
room, the adults thinking of blood.

Grandmother, falcon on a stool,
perches for Mom to call.
She'll be at her wrist,
minding the morphine drip,
comfort struggling in her beak.

        By now, we know;
        we know, but when.

Mom's breathing is unwinding. She is still
in the chair, still alive—but soon
a China Doll in a pink box—silent
to the bullets' reports and Spanish retorts
from the Zenith. Guitar, guns, a single turtle,
Mexicans running. English subtitles
eat the TV. Pops' eyes
fight between the screen and his dying wife.

        By now, we know;
        we know, but when.

Someone dies on screen again: suddenly
gripping roses to his shirt. But really,
he's been dying since the film began,
waiting for his cue to lurch,
to stiffen and fall, tripping over something

somehow invisible until now. I explain
the death. Its artistic merit. When the last words fail
the screen, black has its way, consuming
light, the TV snows its black and white, the room fills.

The tape needs rewinding. Blood climbing back
home into each chest, guns swallowing back
bullets, whole sentences unwrite
as words bury themselves in throats
and what I know recoils:

I would
not have stood. I would not
have walked
between Grandmother, Pops,
where Mom breathes
and the tubes somehow
invisible until now.
I lurch
Mom stiffens Pops starts Grandmother
swoops snow falls my fist balls at her

   I mutter *I know.*

And it snows in the room with what I know.
The adults need subtitles. I don't
explain, rewind. My fist a new alphabet,
some alien's mouth they don't understand. But

      really, Mom's been waiting
since the film began.

"Douglas," she says.

See me, Mom? I'm writing
the subtitles. I'm trying to rewind.
These words are melting;
nothing comes back.

Discount Ritual In 4 Parts: "Bag Of Afro"

afro	on	skull
skull	wrap	brain
brain	hatch	dreds
dreds	come	calling
calling	me	dred
dread	catch	brain
brain	wrack	skull
skull	shed	afro
afro	in	bag

afro in bag
      "you gonna keep that?"
afro in bag
      "yeah   for remembering"
afro in bag
      could be used against me
afro in bag
      someone working both hands!!!
afro in bag
      in closet   with katana
afro in bag
      in box with stories
      of devil deals in pool halls
      nightmares in barbershops
      & a voodoo kitchen

      & hoodoo in kitchen
& afro in bag
      & matches in kitchen
& afro in pot
      & smoke in kitchen
& afro in flames
      & cinders in sink

& the apartment stink
        like hoodoo gone bad
& the apartment stink
        like secrets let out
& the apartment stink
        with the fear of it all

Auto

I feel I could eat women.

Driving alone, I'm hungry,
hawking bus stops and sidewalks.

Eyeballs grinding, I harden.

My mind, a bulging ice box.
My computer, a deep freeze.

This bingeing grows out of hand—

my wastebasket coughing up
the napkins hiding the bones.

Show It!!!

Here is a truth about pornography #1
nipple is nipple
and juts from no
melon on no vine,
no light from no sedan.
it is NO made YES. made.

Here is a truth about pornography #2
GOD! some of them like it
some GOD! of them like it
some of them GOD! like it
some of them like it GOD!

but they better

                    not

                            . . . show it!!!

Here is a truth about pornography #3
the rectum can become a skull's socket
with what it sees. oh but
the rectum cannot become any thing but rectum.
find my eye full of rectum.
my skull's socket
becomes something else it cannot.

Here is a truth about pornography #4
choice of woman is a fast food choice.

a redhead is a chicken sandwich with catsup.
a blonde is a chicken sandwich with mustard.
a brunette is a chicken sandwich with soy sauce.

I have chosen chicken because I have made my choice.
I choke. my chicken is deep in my throat.
I choke and my fist moves at my gut.
I vomit and mop it off with my sandwich's hair.
(but a sandwich shouldn't have hair in it!)   I have made—
I return to the menus   —my choice

Here is a truth about pornography
NO I like it   I don't but I do it
sometimes GOD! YES I have
choice.   oh but I choke.

. . . Miles was guilty of self-confessed violent crimes against women such that
we ought to break his records, burn his tapes and scratch up his CDs
until he acknowledges and apologizes . . . —Pearl Cleage

The trumpet's mouth is apology. —Terrance Hayes

You just—?. . . Write a poem about your need to do that. —Amaud Jamaul Johnson

"LIVE/EVIL"

the pin's point   comes down on the butterfly.
the knuckle   comes down on Ms. Cicely.
the mallet   comes down on the CD case.

                               [wait]

the mallet   comes down on the butterfly.
the pin's point   comes down on Ms. Cicely.
the knuckle   comes down on the CD case.

                               [a]

the knuckle comes down on the butterfly.
the mallet comes down on Ms. Cicely.
the pin's point comes down on the CD case.

                               [bit]

the pin's point the knuckle the mallet

                               [dammit]

the butterfly Ms. Cicely the CD case

                       !!!!!!

    the rose's velvet plumes rip at the aphids' spit— /but that feeds something.
    the phoenix's dazzling petals in the ash dross— /but that births something.
    the martyr's ecstatic smile as the bowels give— /but that saves something.

        what did we make?

listen to the butterfly, the pin point makes no sound
sticking the felt shell. no brass wail into the air. hear
it silent as a necktie. this isn't quite right. Ms. Cicely a CD case?
and the pin-stripe 3-piece—did he wear a pin-stripe 3-piece?
did she kiss its lapel with red lipstick? did he stick her lips red?
did she kiss it? I threw out the liner notes, I don't know, I don't know!

sometimes he wore a pin-stripe 3-piece and a dazzling tie.
the air was what bowels give. I have a mallet.

did he kiss her   lips red?   did he stick her
with a pin's point?   listen to the brass wail.

                    listen to the butterfly!
the plastic breaks
                    and the silent breaks   this is the song of a man
thinking he can build a rose with a mallet,
          make an infant phoenix with a pin's point,
          be a martyr with knuckles.   this is the song of a man
          who threw out the liner notes,   he wore ash dross.
     wait a bit,
                    dammit*!!!!!!* Ms. Cicely
                                        why won't you wait? listen
                                   to the song of a man
giving   what bowels give. he had   a mallet and
the oils in the hands cripple   the butterfly
                         won't fly again, so,
                         butterwait. butterstay. butterstill.
     my fists are felt.   SHIT! what have we made?
                         better wait   stay still!!!!!! listen
                              to the song of a man
          in its 3-piece shell.   it comes down,
                                                        it comes down.

the pin's point   the knuckle   the mallet
                                        [wait a bit]
no birthing   no saving   no feeding
                    dammit listen
                              to the song of a man who breaks.

               what have we made*???!!*

25

"THE JET ROAR SAYS"

Poem With Some Sand And All At Once—Shaitan!

At the edge of it, you're in the middle of it.
        The sea steady shushes this,
each shell scalloped over the grits and grains.
This is exactly what they said it'd be like over here:
        [the sea whispering behind] you take some home
in your shoes, towel. Each shell some shill playing with itself.
This is Southern California, but it's CALIFORNIA™. It's a game after all!

You and your bucket, it's a game:
                scoop and flip—a parapet, a game of it—
                on your towel, flipping fortifications
                of sand. A coastline of citadels. And the game,
          you Godzilla, Godzilla
                    is to destroy it.

              *   *   *   *

At the edge of it, you're in the middle of it.
        The jet roar tells you this,
each shell scalping the grunts and groans.
This is exactly what they say it's like over there:
        [the jet roar says] if you go home
with your self in a towel, it's because you didn't listen to the jets.
This is Southern California, but it's "Iraq." It's a game after all!

You and your musket, it's a game:
                aim and fire—a turret, a game of it—
                on your belly, blasting fortifications
                of sand. The sand is mined but not yours. And the game,
          you God/killer, God/killer
                    is to liberate it . . .

              *   *   *   *

At the edge of it, you're in the middle of it.
        The brochures hate this,
each shell scaping the grottoes and grades.
This is exactly what they say it's like living over there:
        [the brochure winks] if you buy a home
you'll cum in a towel, because it's so good here—did you see the lake?
This is Southern California, but it's "Provence." It's a game after all!

You and your wallet, it's a game:
                tour and buy—an investment, a game of it—
                on your credit, financing fortifications
                of sand. The sand is now yours. And the game,
           you good dealer, good dealer
                  is to profit!!!!!!!

                  *   *   *   *

At the edge of it, you're in the middle of it.
        The cacti remind you of this,
each shell scaling the grittiest of grains.
This is exactly what they say it's like dying over there:
        [the cacti rasp] if you don't know the way home,
throw in the towel, because it's so hot here, you didn't see a lake.
This is Southern California, but it's wasteland. It's a game after all!

You and your gullet, it's a game:
                burn and die—a remnant, a game of it—
                on your last breath, cursing fortifications
                of sand. You are now the sand's. And the game,
           you God-fearer, God-fearer
                  is to survive it?

                  *   *   *   *

        (Sand is tricky, it is poor counterfeit water. Pour
      counterfeit water into a glass. It is sand, even the glass:
        which is clear as water but is sand. Clear?

Sand is trickly, counterfeit water poured through pores
into glass; which is water? Is it sand, the glass even?
Poor water in a clear glass. But is sand clear?)

* * * *

Come pick through the sand, infants and old men. Search for shells,
search for coins, all the treasures of your postcard dreams. Say: *Mine!*

You there, be Godzilla! You there, wash your feet before you get in the car.
Say: *I love it here*. There are bodies everywhere. And drive-thrus. Succulent!
Here is a camera, a carbine, a canteen, a carport—
at the edge of it? You're in the middle of it. It's just like they say.

Sand is tricky. Clear?

*
* *
*

Shaitan!

Sam'!

Shaitan!

Harmattan!

Sim'!

Kham'!

Shaitan!

*

Come pick through the limbs of infants,
pluck the prickly pears of toes of fingers
purple as plums—do you hear a jet?

There are bodies everywhere—bury each in a newspaper
and give them to an eagle with eyes plucked. God, it'll be a sight!
Something for his scrapbook,
a postcard written in crude:

"Went to the beach
and drove to the base
at Twenty Nine Palms,
saw lovely model homes
then headed to Death
Valley—all in one day!

Wish you were here."

The gila monsters are drinking atomic milk
and the cacti have stopped hiding their pistolas!

The bullets sizzle in flight and the sun whispers hoodoo.
The desert empties its shoes and waits at a broken shower.
Dude—is that skateboard made of bone? Whose? What's? *May I*

take your order? A muezzin buzzes—a cow is being offered up.
The drive-thru is bulletproof—your house keys chatter
like stowaways in a minivan. The milk-fed gila monsters
are big as camels and come with optional technology
nooks and two-way fireplaces. There are bodies everywhere.

Say *I love it here!*

Close your Venetian blinds. There's an old man
with a mail order metal detector.
He wants a rare nickel and knows the sand hordes such things.
The trickle-down sand. Dreaming of springs and hoarding
enough nickels to pay the mortgage. To build a lake. To eat a lake. *Yes. Give me*
a lake—super size it! The jets roar. The cacti seem to fire all at once—
someone's found a shell in the sand.

Say *Mine!*

There is metal all over now. A boy rolls around on hot bony wheels—
Dude—is that—? His shoes empty. The monsters grow. The eagle
whispers hoodoo. The shower breaks.

THE ORANGE ALERT

Picture the upturned millipede, dead,
        and see the streets of Altadena:
palm tree rows against the concrete, stiff
        to the horizon.
There have been no birds big enough,
        we are comforted, to pluck
the chitins from before our yards
        and vanish
into the sun like dog-fighting MiGs.
        War bears litters of similes.

Altadena, smog hugs the foothills like mustard gas
        where our rich peer through their blinds
into ravines, Santa Anas sway the mustard plants, yuccas
        bob, some man—his cigarette,
a full gas-can, an itch. We've known
        the orange alert, fires reaching for helicopters
like cartoon cats clawing at panicked birds.

Yesterday, fire engines and HAZMAT trucks
        jostled at Alameda and El Molino
like beetles eating a four-legged spider.
        That morning, radios warned of orange.
Neighborhood kids watched officers climb in
        and out an open manhole,
consulting the entrails of the great dead millipede.
        We watched the ground;
the sun hotter than all year.
        The mountains hid Santa Anas,
The smog went orange with dusk, the growing shadows
        of lingering birds.

America, no brass bands,
No confetti. Please
Put away your pinwheels
& tin whistles.
—Yusef Komunyakaa

ANTHEM (COLLAPSING)

i. twwwwweeeeeeeeeeeeettttt!!!!!!!!!
the drum major jabbing his mace
into the crust of rhythm

claiming the moon with color and cloth:

to thee I sing.

ii. song of sam
graffiti the sky with your jetstreams,
sign your name with neon gunpowder;
fire works wonders on the façade,
squatter's rites to your heaven.

your eyes peering lusty
from a zillion televisions,
errant Argus in a garish tuxedo,
top hat full of dead rabbits.
make them all disappear.

your pink bayonet finger,
the sirens in your glare,
hoary glory knotted in your beard,
clockwork shadows of danger
egg the brushstrokes at your torso,
that stubborn white background thrust
up your heart like a puppeteer's fist,
nails urging your toothy servos.

what you want
is children of your own.

not the hoodwinked nephews and nieces,
your spit-shined favorites.
nor those you beat yourself into
'til their skulls open like hymen,
accepting your rocket ships,
monuments and torpedos.

you, who hand out tampered
candy at reunions, your zany
suit, your marble eyes.

all your gifts rotting
beneath the heat of your pockets.
the balloons you offer, collapsing.

iii. threnody for haliæetus leucocephalus
feathered scud clutching nightshade
and barbed bolts. white-headed
predator clad in American-made Teflon vest
resting in a twisted nest on high. eyes
scanning the dust for prey. spraying
guano in the uplifted face of hope:

may you remain endangered.

iv. ballot booth slowgrind
baby whyyyy caint yoo jus see it my way
oooooooh if yoo cd jus let me in
why wont cha hear what I gots to say
I promise IIIII never tell no lies, suga

honey yoo know IIIII do it good to ya
I git it riiiiiight all day&night
jus let me in ya know IIIIIll do ya
jus say the word & IIIIIIIma work it out

baby whatcha waitin for
the answer is clear to me
forget them ones that came before
IknowIknowyouknow you dear to me

cmon baaaaaaby
jus let me iiiiiiiiiiiiiin

v. melting pot (original dance mix)
the sausagemen are lifting their war grins & casting lots
& carving names into the soil & greasing their torpedos
& not going off record & the tvs agree with all the
newspapers & pinstriped editors price shiny new yachts

& people are picking sides & they don't all pick yours
& bomb shelters pregnant w/sweat vomit fear onto main street
& storefronts surrender their glass eyes to bricks their guts
to the talons of hyenas & the police shoot & shoot & shoot

somebody start the shuttles! cry the soccer moms packing
their children into tupperware & the fatcats jam their hearts
into ice trays & write checks to scientists the bus depots
are jammed w/pariahs & funk & the cornfields sprout rifle

muzzles & the flags of stillborn nations god bless americaaaaaaaa
megaphones knifefight in the wings of skyscrapers & pamphlet
orgies writhe on sidewalks the prophets of doom cash
their reality checks laughing all the way to the bank &

tshirt wolfpacks cross piss at ruptured hydrants & the crack
houses are empty & the fiends are seeing dragons & navy seals
are wearing bandannas & flannel & the priests have climbed
into rocketships & the pimps haven't picked up their dry cleaning

& the 747s stab toward the hospitals & the ghettos are spreading
gonorrhea from backflipping 40 oz & wall street fills its sepulchre
& the president crosses all the airwaves like hope in a sharp suit &
the president goes to the mic which looks like a sword stuck in a slab

of asphalt & looks out at the amber waves purple mountains shining seas
pulls out a black box & reads a suicide note to the world that says
sorry we couldn't keep everything yankee doodle dandy

vi. theme from star wars (remix)
everybody knows
THEY got stuff in the sky.

patriotic meteors and
cosmic supersoldiers

with worldwide
drop zones,

razor blade parachutes,
licenses to kill,

maps to each of our homes,
our social security numbers

and bombs bursting behind their eyes.

look:

a dangling satellite
eyeballs the globe's ripe ass.

earth's teeth feel
rain coming.

and the fateful lightning

git loose

for Keota
AT THE PINK TEACUP

                    Keota cuts sweet tea with talk
the room empty but for us the brother waiting and love songs

later he'll recall tanks from a stoop carve a sonnet
of the day no one was underground in New York

as if the sky needed holding up and everyone came out
to help   he'll pay for our food and we'll stare

from the stoop as attachés commute past the swollen
garbage bags flowering in dusk   but now he's talking about love

his tongue a knife he cools in free refills the menu says
we shouldn't get   he's talking about what he wants

how he wishes it wouldn't burn his grandfather down
or that brothers would remember how fickle the Bible is

and the brother at The Pink Teacup is refilling our glasses   he smiles
like it's the easiest thing in the world and the menu looks stupid

and petty   later Keota will talk about gas masks and fruit stands
how all he could do was cuss the man who looked

like some glass-eyed insect buying apples *you're scaring*
the kids you fucking asshole and how scared he is

of what happens when everyone looks to the sky
for messages and keeps everything sweet

somewhere cold   New York will offer us bouquets in black plastic
the menus will fold commuters will buy apples and forget their gas masks

in the closet   right now Keota isn't talking about love   the knife is in his hand
cutting salmon croquettes   he doesn't want to burn his people down   but later

he'll talk about Sikh women beaten in Harlem   the bumper stickers
and flags flying past us as we watch brothers hoop in a cage   before then

he'll talk about what brothers do once they find out   he is full of sweet
tea and pink flesh   the brothers full of sweat argue over fouls   the cage fence

full of spectators like flies on the black garbage bags   the fruit stands
full of apples some bruised as the Sikh women and New York

full of bumper stickers crawls back underground scrambles for its love songs
Bibles tanks gas masks   Keota wishes people would remember how fickle the Flag is

and right now he is talking about love   when the brother comes back
with the pitcher Keota is through   later he will love the brothers   he pays now

"LOVE 'EM TO DEATH"

The KKK held a rally in Saint Paul, Minnesota, August 25, 2001.

RALLYING

i. ghost stories
tomorrow, white men pull skins from linens,
drift the Mississippi, ghosts of magnolia trees.

my wife imagines 30 dim rednecks. lame
shotgun hounds leashed in frayed knots.

I know better: the stairs before the capitol
buried in waxen blossoms.

ii. chicken
picking through
bones on my plate:

chicken. I plot escape routes,
she argues we should be

at the rally. bones pile.
my teeth

are tearing dark meat:
why do you want to go?

my tone, bare,
warning "White Only."

iii. static
the car doors slam
and foul things leave

my throat. I shut off
the pop rap radio station,

embarrassed to hear another
black man spout bullshit.

iv. dares
no haunted house on my block. no haints
waiting in basements. no windows to look through

on dares: stupid antics for eking scuffed manhood.
had there been, I would have hidden like one ducks torches

weaving between poplars, big boys just dying:
there ain't no ghosts! only folks in sheets.

v. rallying
tonight, we approach the dark
capitol. caught on a dead end street,

I change direction, hurling
my lopsided terror to the headlights.

we stare at it. the motor stutters.
Nicole says we don't have to go

tomorrow. I drive forward. a phantom dies
under the wheel, a rolling drum.

vi. jump. start.
morning. parking lot. I pay
for being too careful. headlights drained my car,

a beaten black thing. I wave
for help. I need to jump

start. to the passing white man or woman,
it must be easy to believe I would pretend

to borrow some power, just to steal, hurt or worse.
lucky an older sister sees me pushing:

same thing happened to me, she says.
the engine turns over.

vii. preparation
I've hidden something hard in a black
umbrella, in case of weather.

viii. race
the exits from home to Saint Paul
fall into the rear view,

every car with white passengers
sears red streaks in my periphery

as we go forward. it seems, so far,
the Klan is winning.

ix. pot
huge puppets entreat the crowd, pastors
in a fevered dream. college kids clamor pots

with hammers. the red shirts sickle
among teamsters, trading flyers. about the green,

a foam of whites scream at their skin-
headed and hooded kin, demonstrating.

Nicole points at what we should take
with us. my camera blinks. holding

their guns at hushed attention, National Guardsmen
wait for us to remember how close we all are.

how much we want from each other.

Triptych: Kitchen

cut
if Rastus slid Tara on the slant
of a flashing cleaver,
blended Rhett's scarlet insides
with remnants of pig and onion
in a single ginsu, Bantu slice,

whose face would peer out
from Cream of Wheat boxes?
whose bright grin
would bring cold whites comfort?

winnowing
they came for Ben last night.
claimed he dipped his spoon
in Miss Annie's pots.
Ben, who smiled while he built
white children with rice for rivets.

they tore down the walls
of his cardboard shack.
threshed him good
before their torches
finished the work.

theirs was a hunger:
as always, Ben served.

batter
at first, Jemima didn't make flapjacks like that.

once they were black as buckwheat
and a blackstrapped stack could crack
the brittle white dishes.

it wasn't 'til master spilled milk in her bowl
did she make those yellow things.

much easier to swallow.

(here is a couplet resolving black love
neatly with a fish you will read later)

. . . and the business of diamonds   sweat   teeth
of flesh (as) ebony mahogany teak
                                        trees falling

away with that hoary eurocentric love
of trees and fall   faces rouged
                                                (like)
                              apples   cherries

GO ON   GIT!!!! swing low mango   cassava
dip the robins   in bebop
                              in boombap

ahhhhh the volta

this is a poem about love in the projects
a projection thereof and what that stripped wallpaper reveals
about nakedness in the face of <u>b</u>ullets <u>b</u>ills <u>b</u>ase   (B-B-B=<u>B</u>OOM)
so this is a poem about love made in a rally about the projects
called:

LOVEPOEM POR DE-FAMILIAR

about burning the gardens
bum rushing the dianthus
the dirty scansion
                        of a begonia
                              a carnation
                                    then a rose!

                        arise my duppy   my zombie   my crackhead
                        travel ye in fours   oh! here's a shock white haint
                        make yourselves rhyme   sway on the downbeat

but this is a poem about sticky LOVE
(how the ink is black + juicy)
quick   a simile for lips (should suggest
sweet and salty) . . . . candied herring
                                        perhaps flushed
                                        with fishnet passion?

{EPIGRAPH . . . *but a sweet old fashioned notion* . . .}

I love my black people   o my Jo'burg
                                        my Trenchtown
                                        my DC
                                        love em to death

tonight's black people have all read "Othello"
and transcripts from the OJ trial
and the sun loves us as Santa Claus loves us
                              red coat
                              black soot
                              green holly
(what's that in his bag??????)
what's Santa without no chimneys?

BACK TO THE PROJECTS
and count to 14

I say this is about love:

               "your skin is so _____"

ATOMIC BUCKDANCE

Note: Atomic Buckdance
should be read as a
crossroads of voices
and values.

Each type treatment
represents a different
figure.

SMALL CAPS:
the two-head

roman italics:
the singer

roman:
the griot

ROMAN CAPS ITALICS:
the victim

ROMAN CAPS:
the authority

BOLDFACED SMALL CAPS:
the trickster

ELECTRIC PORCHES(SPOTLIGHT)
FANFARE SLINGSHOT ME TOO AIR WAVES
FLEX MY BLINGSPAN & BE MOVIN ON UP

TO CAT CALLIN CAMERAS   CHIMERA COONIN
A NEON MYTHOS CHANT(IN) CATHODES
HALLOWED VIDEOS PLATINUM HALOES BEZELED AURAS

DRIZZLE SCORES FROM STEREO LIPS GLOSSED TIL
THE CENTER FOLDS & MY BACKBONE SLIP

gon rip stars like supah nova cane grippin solar pimp

like sugah cane grippin pimp liftin megawatt spot sol

got harems of drums lickin my feet

got boudoirs of brass sayin   my name

i be the softshoe shah shakin 14 karat salt

dance the shine off a dime

teeth full of primetime

& WHEN I DIE ANGELS W/GOOD HAIRGONNA TURN MY BONES INTO SLOW GRINDS
SAY WHEN I DIE GOOD HAIR ANGELS GONNA SLOW GRIND MY BONES

(PAIR O DICE ROLE [CRAP-OUT] / PROMISE LANDS OUTFIELD
NOT QUITE THE RUN HOME / WE X-SPECTRED
STILL RUNNIN THE BASIS OF BLACKLIFE) make sure you juke right

ALL ABOARD BLACK BACKS
DOE SEE DOE

CRAWL

ABHORRED BLACKS BACK TO BUCK

JELLY ROLL IN SHIP BELLY SWOLE W

SWEATY RHYTHM

51

eeny meeny miney mo

CAN'T YOU HEAR THE RATS SCRATCHIN THEY WAY OUT OF MY SHOES

catchanigger by the toe

CLAWIN THE HULL OF MY SHOES

if he hollers let im go.

OVER

BOARD BLOCKS: BUCK DON'T SEE DOUGH
MONEY THRONE TWO FEET
SMILE FOR BLUE EYE SPOT LIGHT
STAGE NAME FOR NEXT STAGE
dance or the critics'll kill ya

GO ON

BACK TO BUCKS

lindy hoppin the flatfoot dum dums

mashin potatoes through starvation

poppin locked glass ceilings

bouncin to the heads of banks

bouncin booties   NEVER CHECKS

CHARGE CARDS ARE LIGHTENING BOLTS

I AM REVERSED LIGHT   BUILDING A BETTER DARKIE

I AM REMIXING LIGHT IN THE CALDRON OF MY SPITSHINE

IT'S TIME FOR NUKE JUKE GRINDS

TIME TO MINE PLATINUM FROM THE FINGERS OF MY RHYTHM

TO FIND DIAMONDS IN MY HOLY TURBO TOEJAM

NO MA'AM I WASN'T GON KEEP IT I WAS GON GIVE IT TO THE WORLD they gonna build satellites that say: that nigga sho can dance

THEY GUNNA BUILD SADDLES

LIGHT THAT NIGGA SHOW

GO ON

NIGGA ANGELS WITH LIPS LIKE WINGS

GONNA SING BACK-UP

PM GONNA SAY BACK UP

WIPE MY FEET ON THE SPOT LIT WELCOME MAT

GONNA CLOSE THE DOOR BEHIND ME

YOU GONNA GO SO LOW?

PM SHAKIN SALT FROM MY POCKETS

TO THE GROUND

LIKE A WEAPON

BLUE-SHAPED FOOTSTEPS ON THE STAGE S

STRAIGHT TEETH   CANON MUZZLE FLASHES

OFF THE STAINLESS STEEL WHOLE NOTES

THE "STAINLESS" STEAL WHOLE NOTES

go on

THEY BURN YOUR FLASH IN THEY PANS

TURN UP THE HEAT

I SHOW CAN KEEP A BEAT

LORD KNOWS MY FEATS IS SORE

53

DANCE ON HEADS OF BROADCAST ANTENNAS W/BOOTYSHAKE ANGELS

DANCIN ON BROADCAST NEEDLES W/ BOOTYSHAKE ANGELS

DANCIN ON BROADCASTE NEEDLES AT BOOT-SHAPED ANGLES

DANCIN NEEDLESS ANGLE

TANGLIN BOOT LACES INTO NOOSE KNOTS

SAVE THAT SHIT FOR TOMORROW

I AIN'T GON BE LEFT BEHIND DRAINED OF JUICE

FLACCID COTTON IN MY NAPS

A NIGGA ANGEL FLAPPIN MY WINGS

I'M OILIN MY WINGS W/BATHTUB GENEROSITY

SCRUBBIN THE BLACK OUT & RISIN WHITE AS ASHES

I'M GON DANCE THE SHINE

OFF A DIME TEETH FULL OF PRIMETIME

YOU WAS SMART YOU'D STOWAWAY

ON STAGE W/ME

"WAITING FOR SOMETHING TO SPILL"

The Chitlin Circuit

NIGGERSHINES NIGGERSHINES A PIECE

NIGGERSHINES NICKEL EACH

FIVE CENT EACH

NIGGERSHINES NIGGER SHINES

INDIANABAMASSOURI

GEORGIADAMICHIGINIAS

BOOT SHAPED TRAINS SHIMMY TRACKS
BRUTE APE BLACKS SHIMMY BRAINS

PENNSYLLINOISOWA

WISCONCINEESSEVANA

BLUES ACTS PAINT SHIMMY RAGE
BRUISE TRAINED BLACKS SHIMMY SHAKE

MINNESOTARKANSASSIPPI

NEWYOKLAHIOLINAS

BREW STAINED STAGE SHIMMY SPACE
BOOT SHAPED TRAINS SHIMMY TRACKS

DAKOTEXORADORNIA

NEBRASKENTUCKYLAND

THE POET AS SETTING

The jolt that comes to bones inside a tumbled streetcar

is what the painter considers as she strokes her-
self into story. There is less to the jolt that

comes as he shuts his eyes before the monitor, save

what he imagines—a lightning bolt, a god tapping
the shoulder. He imagines the sky swelling

with ceiling fans or the guano of extinct birds,

a jolt riding from his shoulder
blades to his eyelids, dropping with roller

coaster clacks to his fingers. Here, he dreams of Frida

Kahlo. Here, he says, *let me spread my flesh out like a*
table linen, let my bones be silver that touches,

making, again, that clack. My skull will be a glass,

set properly, I have class enough. What jolt is
it to chew over class, his body set before him as

a reader sips (perhaps) a glass of something heady? We give

books spines, we break them. The table will have
its legs, its head. The body is upon us. Does the table have

a stomach? Is it simply there to bear our hunger

without its own, like a eunuch bathing a stripper?
What is the poet without eyes or ears—reading, listening? He is

a platform—a place to set, that to set it with. And if this is

all, what will he do when the reader finishes a glass,
rises from the poet's head, and passes

into the city? Covered with a linen, he is waiting for

something to spill, perhaps a girl in Mexico rolling
her ankle in a street-

car.

(DIG!) BLOOM IS BOOM, SUCKA!

OPENING CREDITS: At first, you think it's a flower, but it's an explosion

Lay lines, lay lines (deep
in the earth where the power's at)
Lay lines below the black lacquer,
black lacquer street (. . . where

the power's at). Back
fire mighty, mighty Brougham
Drop the big trash bin trash man. Spill
the silver, dope fiend,

spill it all over
the black lacquer street. You hear me?
I see you! That's my eye under
this hat. Come again,

Brougham! Let's walk, now.
Under this big hat. Storms slip off
the rooftops, wash everything
Ripple red. Now drop

the big bin. Dig me
done in Ripple red. Dig me done
in red pose under this big hat.
Let's walk, now. This shit—

—for Baby Doll

ACT 1: At first, they think I'm a flower, but I'm an explosion

In the end: gun smoke
and Merlot. In the end:
a white man in a river.
In the end: trash bins in the green.
In the end: all of the names involved.

In between: KUNG FU!
In between: Naugahyde!
In between: Sookie! Sookie!
In between: Baby Doll catch it!

Why you catch it Baby Doll?!

WHY YOU ALWAYS CATCH IT BABY DOLL?!

This shit for Baby Doll. This shit—

Spill the silver, dope fiend. A storm
of spoons and forks, you hear? Diddy

the lay lines. Seedy seedy city.
Downtown billboards, Uptown graffiti!
Expect a Deuce packed with ax handles,
with ball bats, with switchblades. Expect blue
Deuce packed with Jack's vandals, with hard cats,
with inmates. Deuce strut.
                    Deuce crawl.
                           Deuce stop.
I see you.

KUNG FU!

Ripple red.

This—

—shit for Baby Doll!

ACT 2: At first, I thought she was flowers, but she was an explosion

Cookin in the kitchen, tea kettle done.
Old lady sweepin the stoop, sweepin the
sweepin the stoop. Tea kettle done. Sweepin
the stoop. Tea kettle done. Cookin. Hear me?

Oh, Baby Doll. It's all about you Baby Doll.
Talk sweet. Look sweet. Talk mean. Look mean.
You the real deal, Baby Doll. No other for me.
Some look like you, but ain't you.
Some talk like you, but ain't you.
Some act like you, but ain't you.

Baby Doll a gunshot in a Lover's Lane!
Baby Doll a guitar chord in a choir robe!
Baby Doll a hot curve in a yellow fog!
Baby Doll a lay line deep in a whirlpool!

Baby Doll—a gunshot! Baby Doll catch it
and spill out Merlot on the Naugahyde.

WHY YOU ALWAYS CATCH IT, BABY DOLL?!
You always catch it.
WHY YOU ALWAYS CATCH IT, BABY DOLL?!

Where my heat? Baby Doll hot curve
spill out. The black lacquer streets
(. . . the power . . .). Where my line? Hear
me? Walk. The sun in the clotheslines
like a red bathmat. Sun in the clotheslines
playin a guitar chord. Where my heat?

Come again, Brougham.
The trash man and the dope fiend
droppin and spillin. Back fire
and big hat. The black

lacquer streets (Where . . .). This
shit for Baby Doll! This shit for—

—Baby Doll

ACT 3: At first, they think it's flowers, but it's an explosion

Jungle on a skillet. Jungle jook slow on a skillet.
Big Jungle little jungle jookin. Hear me? Down below
the down below a pit. Junkies simmer. Dancin dime tight

with white man's White Lady. Stainless steel smoke
nod the nod with White Lady. Down below

pull my coat to Baby Doll? The nod the. What you know about
Baby Doll down below a pit the down below black lacquer
(... the pow ...) nod the nod. Who hit Baby Doll (YOU ALWAYS CATCH IT)?

Slow grind dime tight with White Lady, Junkies simmer,
on a skillet jook faster. Big little jook, hear

me? Flip the pot, silver spill! The nod. Jook stop!
What you know about Baby Doll (YOU ALWAYS
CATCH IT)? Pit a flop, simmer still, Junkies sleep

don't know jack about Baby Doll (WHY YOU ALWAYS ...)
jook with White Lady, know jack about Baby

Doll. White Lady a gunshot in a black lacquer street.
(Where the power ...). Smoke down a pit. White man's
junkies don't know jack about Baby Doll. Where my heat?

Back to black lacquer.
The mighty Brougham back fire.
The spilling silver. The dropping
bin. This shit for Ba—

—by Doll

ACT 4: At first, I thought they were flowers, but there was an explosion

Unbalanced coin-op washer wobble. Squeejee on the glass
squeal over street preach spiel. Sink drip to the pot lid. Wobble
washer, squeejee squeal spiel. Sink. Drip. Lid. Drip. Lid. Drip. Hear me?

Red light on the black lacquer
                    (deep in . . .), red light
wink and flophouse chatter
                    o, o. . . ! Corner stone foxy,
vinyl brick house. Red light air
                    got dollars in it.
Dollars in the nylon, bur-
                    ied in the black o, o. . . !
lacquer street (deep in the earth.
                    Where the power?) Mack
and his loud hat, his leopard
                    loud hat, red light air. Pockets, foxy.

What Mack know about Baby
                    Doll? Don't know . . .
Mack know corner stone foxy:
                    Ain't Baby Doll,
but it feel . . . Ain't Baby
                    Doll, but it sound . . . Mack
sell a vinyl brick house. Dig me
                    done o, o. . . ! The red light
air, chatter, what Mack know
                    got dollars in it. Ain't Baby Doll.
Dig me done o, o. . . !
                    leopard loud, squeal, the pot lid.
Flophouse and red
                    light wink. What you know about? Dig
me. Wink. Baby o, o. . . ! unbalanced
                    coin op—a lover's lane, a gunshot in it! NO

Merlot on the black lacquer, black lacquer
street (. . . the earth . . .) This shit for Baby Doll!
This shit—KUNG FU! Wobble. Sink. Mack's jacked
leopard hat on the black lacquer street (. . .) spiel

Drip

Drip

Drip

Drip

Silver spill catchin the red light wink.

This shit for baby—

—doll.

ACT 5: At first, he thought I was flowers, but I was an explosion

Army of Broughams, backfire. Mighty,
mighty. Trash bin platoon drops a platoon of trash bins. Silver spill,
waterfall of silver spill, thousand fiends with wet hands. Spill. This shit
for Baby Doll WHY YOU ALWAYS CATCH IT?!

Mansion in the green, the green hilltop. Far from the black lacquer
black lacquer street (. . . the power's at). Dig me done in creep.
That's my eye under the shadow. Let's walk in creep. Past the gate,

watchdogs in suits cockblock the walk. Gorillas in suits. Expect
KUNG FU! Ripple red. Suits bent funny. Moon
a white man's face. Moon over mansion in the green. Let's walk up

the hilltop. Spill, you hear me? Spill a river of silver, fiends.
Moon in the balcony, behind lattice
sky. Moon in the balcony, lattice sky, lattice sky. What you

know about Baby Doll? Moon in the balcony, before a
filigree drape. Moon in the balcony,
filigree drape, filigree drape. What you know about Baby

Doll? Moon don't know jack about Baby Doll. Moon knows balcony.
Dig me up the stairs, a platoon of trash
bins, hear me? This shit for Baby Doll. Backfire—

{*In the end: gun smoke and Merlot. In the end: a white man in a river. In the end: trash bins in the green. In the end: all of the names involved.*}

—Brougham. Drop

the bin. Spill silver on the black lacquer street.

Lay lines (where the power's at). This shit for Baby Doll.
Some talk like you, but ain't you.
Some act like you, but—

—ain't you.

CLOSING CREDITS: At first, we thought they were flowers, they were explosions

Hymen Munster as **Hard Cats**
Parry White as **Jack's Vandals**
Deal (w/) it aints as **Inmates**
Nod the nod the as **Junkies**
Bye Baby as **White Lady**
Miss Udder as **Corner Stone Foxy**
H.E.R. as **Vinyl Brick House**
Jam Deaf as **Mack**
Them aka Dem as **Watchdogs/Gorillas in Suits**
Canon Bawla as **White Man**
This shit, Hear me as **Baby Doll**
Douglas Kearney as **The Poet**

"THE MOUTH GULPS THE PUPPET"

The Poet Writes The Poem
That Will Certainly Make Him Famous

0.

the first line? "blackface is sometimes the truth."
the poet knows this will make fire.

ponders performing in some dark room, squinting at the black type—
red gel spots like laser sights from a rifle big as a bus.

but here, the sniper stirs herbal tea, has a cell phone,
the number of a woman the color of thrush wings.

for now: the sniper with the cell phone will be *he*.

he misses the next line beneath the spoon clanging in the mug
like the clapper in a schooner's alarm bell. the third line,

perhaps: "... the smoldering cork testifies ..." or "... the moldy corpse terrifies ..."
he considers each. and wonders about the second line

—then about the girl he saw boarding the bus,
what her name sounds like whispered in a dim room

of red candles, a radio where the poet is. "—ncing and bucking.
and the yes and suh ..."—he misses something else,

the new line of little to do with corks or corpses—courts, maybe—
and what's "... un a gold coin promise, layaway heaven with teeth and silence ...";?

he is lost between a poem, a cell and a thrush's wing.

so by this time the poet should probably place a refrain
as this is going to be a long poem, long enough to make the poet famous.

1.

blackface is sometimes the truth
but with added emphasis. a boldface where
the smoldering cork testifies.

[the issue is intent, nahmean?
like what is *nahmean* when *you see*
knows its way around the alleys
of the tongue? what is *nahmean*, nahmean?
and the intent is the issue, you see?] [nahmean?]

blackface is sometimes a lie
but with added detail. a bold face where
the smoldering cork testifies.

2.

but to what? the sawdust packed pockets, the brogan's salty shadow?
to the straps? scraps off the hips of tin platters?

the train's constant *is a-comin*? the minister's constant *that Someday*
what is the cork, still smelling of cheap wine, some doe-

eyed muscatel, a poor man's dream-color of velvet, some sap
fresh from a cicada tableau to a night club in a Sunday suit,

cardboard under his left sock, the bootblack ache slithering out
above his ass, the bootblack cash kissed in waxy fingerprints

offered up, offered up to the waitress who won't smile for a "what this get?"
the bottle brought back, armpit warm? this cork, tossed to the floor

and kicked, a careless jig swung by a white chick, and rolled below
a table awaiting some jittering negro, whose gig it is to eyeball

these corks, to swoop down, hands a pair of crows, to swoop up
the cork, bear it backstage, to pull it from his pocket like a magician's dove,

transform it into smoke and ovation.

what does this testify?

what is this truth?

why speak of the fire, the first kiss of flame to the cork?

watch *Bamboozled*. that's all *I* did.

what does *this* testify?

3.

what is truth?
again reading
some magazine,

again waiting
for the dressing room
door to open:

fire gleaming off the platter
like a breakfast of stars,
burning cork

from Portugal, and cork
doesn't sink in rough waters,
like fine schooners

from Portugal, and fire
splits the blackness of dark
like the fingers of sailors

from Portugal, whose tongues
teach new tongues to the lips
in the darkness of blacks

from Africa, and burn
the sea into their faces
like smoke in a blue lit

dressing room. and I
close the magazine
full of rappers swimming

in denim, ism smoke
and wait for the door
to open. the embers to ignite

4.

dancing and bucking

spotlight's prison-break eye and the sweat that lifts from the skull
and the pancake sheen allowed for the cameras, the pancake

that will not run, and the clothes that cling to the mouths of wetness
and the red gels that turn the words into spastic ants holding tiny cue cards!!!!!

but the stomach churn of memorization, *no no no*, the revisions on the other
copy in the other notebook in the other room *no no no* the gimpy music stand

tilt, the red eye, the spotlight's stomach, the prison-break sheen, the ants cling,
the pancake mouth, the spastic words, the cameras lift, the clothes' wetness,

the skull tilt, churn
                    turn
                        run
                    no no
                        NO
                        DANCE   BUCK

                    *   *   *   *

the yes and sir

the room.
the books.
hands telling
what I know
to a machine.
alone. dreaming,
yes, dreaming
of pinning myself
to journals like
a prized butterfly.
the ink of my beauty
fading on the white pages.

5.

a rusty bicycle is a copper skeleton against the mattress.
through the chain link, children kneeling on the concrete

look lined for butchering. chewed sedans bleed into the street,
into sewer bellies.

I've written these images too many times. DC is my ghetto—
every black poet should have one, as every white poet should have

a movie-house or a lake. white poets have attractions.

black poets should also have grandmothers.

I have grandmothers—one living, one not. neither mopped
any floor but her own. if I stand on their memories, I am too tall

to be jammed into a tenement. black birds peck at my journals. my fingers
work grime into Elm Place in LeDroit Park, divine urine from Florida Ave

and goad fiends from T Street's throat. these are not my muses.

an adjective. a noun. a simile. "ragged storefronts like beaten wives."

I must imagine what might go on behind bricks, past the railing
climbing up the stoops like wrought iron centipedes. the windows are open

sometimes at night. it was hot,
one black grandmother had a pool. air conditioning. on days without smog,

you could see the sea or someone riding a horse
past the liquor store. no one *needs* horses in Altadena. here,

horses are diamond necklaces. diamond necklaces that shit in crosswalks.
in DC there is a different kind of horse, and I need it for poems as I need ink.

it is not my muse, nahmean? one black grandmother didn't sit in
the back of buses. Raleigh lay before her, already mopped. the crows are waiting

at the edge of the page. see, the madhouse that seeped out into NE
before exploding into panhandlers stranded in phantom ants,

drifting mothers birthing flying dutchmen, that man who walked
all the way to 6th Street swinging a golf club like a white woman dancing—

these are not my muses.
they aren't even mirrors.

they are cork awaiting flame.

                    blackface
                                        IS

sometimes.

6.

the truth: there's a man holding a cell phone to his ear like a seashell.

he is not hearing the ocean—though on a clear day you can see the sea—
but the flutter of thrush wings.

there's someone on a microphone. call him "ocean."

> MAN: *(to cell phone)* —eah,   nah, ain't nobody here.
> he didn't show up.   yeah, it is still early—hold up.
> nah, this nigga's just loud.   what?
> he's aiight, just loud.

> OCEAN: *(just loud)* . . . and silence! let me tell you who I am! let me write it
> in pitch, in slippery shadow! the pages flee from me, like
> fish from a diving bird! I'll use my skin for paper. my feet—

> MAN: *(to cell phone)* —'m leaving in a minute.   ha.   you want me
> to pick up some food?   hummus?   from which place?
> yeah, wait— *(claps)*   —aw shit.   naw, I just thought that nigga
> was done.

7.

it don't stop y'all.

like a ship on a bullwhip wind
like a whip on a broad black back
like a black on a sugar cane row
like a cane on a bent boy's spine
like a boy on a crossing-over walk
like a cross on a weeping woman's breast
like a woman on a blue wave's tongue
like a wave on a dirty shore's shoulder
like a shore on a slope beneath foam

it don't stop y'all. the ocean's belly is full
of women—shadows of children trailing from their ankles

on chains, of men with blood flaring from their throats like ribbons.
the ocean's belly is full of bones. ghost towns of ribcages.
campsites of skulls. railroads of femurs.

how many cities has the ocean swallowed?

how many more will it heave forth,
bones in the sand, picked at by gulls white as sun-bleached sails?

8.

nightmares of cities scrawled in slippery shadows.
the boulevards' sprawls kick like children

being butchered under the gawking stars—*hey!*
someone is pouring transmission fluid into a sewer's mouth,

pushing shipwrecks from a womb, stapling ants to panhandlers,
spritzing piss on everything. are these the city's nightmares

or nightmares of cities? is this—?
                              the poem that will certainly

make the poet famous. sometimes these words are slippery
shadows. this is not a muse. sometimes,

these words are burning cork, near a mirror. blackface is.
sometimes the truth.

9.

I got rivers—lotsa rivers. I got Jordan—who could ask for anything mooooooohhh
O swing————swing it! Swii-I-Iii-IIng low [said swing it on low] 'm talkin bout
that CHAAAAAAAAAaaAriot [bout that chariooooot] LOOK OUT 's swingin low

swingin! [swingin?] SWINGIN [who's swingin?] Joshuaaaaa! Joshuaaaaaaa!
Joshua's swingin [why's he swingin] the Battle [who?] Joshuaaaaaaaaaaa fit the
battle of Je-E-e-EeEricho [Jericho! Jericho!] said JoooshuaAaaA was-a swingin at the
battle of JeEerichoooo [look out UH HUH look out] say he was he was fighting at
that battle at JeE-e-e-Erichooooo [Jericho!] and the walls   came   tum
bling   DOOOOOOOOOOWN!!!

he brought down houses.

hurricanes bumped titties in his wind pipe
and he'd leave the stage with shingles in his hat.

the air in here is neon.

the air in here is a tight dress and pressed collar.

what's left in this juke house bent with blue music?
the banjos stutter like a cheating man. no black face here but what the sun give you.
the corks plug the jugs or skitter ungathered among cardboarded soles.

       this is a postcard from a bucket o' blood:

       black eye stamped and signed with chipped teeth.
       the shimmy caught on film, a blues act painted.

       consider the cruelty of postcards,
       like allowing a starving man to sniff your plate
       through a screen door.

       the bucket o' blood
       is a plate of hemlock and mandrake. what must one hunger for
       to envy this?

there are tourists who wander the nightmares of cities
jamming ragged storefronts into cameras like souvenirs.

there are tourists who go shirtless like ornamental blades out scabbards,
slog down rivers, towing canoes.

there are tourists who descend the gleaming stairs from their jetliners
to camp on the stone pallets of hills,
to watch the Sherpa shepherds hustle the yak
as a picnicker watches ants and fancies
carrying a basket of brie is kinship. what must one hunger for?

and then there, wearing a garland of mosquitoes and a second skin of sweat,
sitting in a tent with a fountain pen and writing—what is the hunger
that says: *I wish you were here*?

                                        10.
here, navy waves toe the dirty shore,
this is what I remember—the actual beach
is like looking at a postcard through a screen door.

seaweed litters the sand like loosened Yaki weaves—
a rusty bicycle color. any Venus born here swims
from a needle and a Styrofoam plate. myth

is an airbrush. so are hymns.
I want to be god-like. Apollo in a Seville with
the sun in the backseat. this is the poem

that will certainly make the poet famous. I write
at night, looking at the stars through the screen, room
fading into light.

let me tell you who I am. let me write it in pitch,
in slippery shadow. the pages flee from me like fish.

11.

question: when a minstrel is born, what should you cook?

> *white man's answer*: a fine kettle of pitch.
> *white woman's answer*: a pot of spoiled oysters.
> *white child's answer*: a banana cream pie.

question: what must a minstrel's hair feel like?

> *white man's answer*: buckshot or cottonseeds.
> *white woman's answer*: beads or latex stubble.
> *white child's answer*: dirty clouds.

question: when a minstrel dies, what should you hang half mast?

> *white man's answer*: his banjo, his bottle cap shoes.
> *white woman's answer*: his trombone, his fiery lipstick.
> *white child's answer*: his kazoo, his greasy halo.

12.
6 collages d'post-moderné visagé noir

8-ball w/a catsup twat

tire w/a breaching welt

coal briquette w/a salmon morsel

tuxedo pants w/a lipstick gash

midnight w/a burning macaw

spilled ink w/blood

13.
what is the cork, stinking of muscatel
like a hammered whore before a trompe l'oeil palace?

the cork is the words.

what is the crimson mouth like a scalloped incision
left oozing into the pressed, white shirt?

the mouth is language.

14.
the words line up like negroes on a Carolina dock

the words line up like squads of freed slaves in the snow

the words line up like a brain trust in a White House photo

the words line up like a circus in a Duluth intersection

the words line up like the offense on a December gridiron

the words line up like Crips before the Hollywood sign

yes sir, sometimes it's truth.
the mouth, you see.

15.
fine poems clamor for metaphor, simile, synecdoche—many
pieces (golf bag-esque, you see)—and live like sequoia. long-

loping verses birthed at a gunshot pass quick as sprinters. sweat?
no good, muscled legs poor bases for sitting at desks.

Muse in her green blouse spreads before the fine poet like suburbs. somewhere
a dove is building a nest, somewhere else, black beaks peck at dead things.

the words line up like woven twigs,
and it wasn't "the moldering corpse" but "the smoldering cork."

the cork is the words.
. . . the pages flee from me like _____

16.
a break for catfish

catfish with mercury from redneck ka-ka
cat at the surface puffin air like tobacco

boot leather skin on em   thick lip grin on em
cat at the surface muddy ripple black shadow
cornmeal cakes on em   salt pepper shakes on em

mercury in catfish from yokel hockey
                gal! strike the pilot light.
                fire's hot! oil's hot!
                keep the meat white,
                gal! scrape off the dark!
mercury in catfish from all that hick shit

2 LBS for $4   4 LBS for 6

17.
the poet orders catfish in Leimert Park,
whose windows bat mud cloth

like fast women's eyelashes
and the old men play chess with stones.

later, when a white man
reads poetry in the black room,

the poet feels something
swim in him, bad as

mercury thrashing in
the mud of his gut.

18.

Mercury was a god of thieves and bottom feeders. in Greece,
he was ghost among cattle, and the ultimate track shoes.

these are stories one could read in college. fine poems
clamor for allusion, the man with the cell phone would hear

illusion, but *he* is one since the poet is not reading this in a red light.
that poem would be: "... skin for paper. my feet dance like two burning

slaves. my spine is a whip and my mouth has stopped working.
I'll use your spit for ink and my tongue for a candle, dancin

and-a buckin. yes and suh ..." but if the poet reads *this* in a red light,
it is no longer illusion. truth is slippery as shadow, as the black

grease from burned cork, slippery as Mercury who was Hermes
but for the empire, nahmean? one could read this in college, too.

19.

HELLO MEMBERS OF THE ACADEMIA

There is that sky, gray as mackerel in a foaming breaker,
Where the wind hushes off the quay
Like line from Uncle Charlie's fly reel ...

84

HELLO MEMBERS OF THE ACADEMIA

Dominguez waiting by the boat, considering
the finger he lost
to the ocean and the wife
he lost to the bourbon. Dominguez
and his hat,
both dirty and beautiful, beaten
into the leaden
photograph
pulling the bar's rafters
down to the seesawed shoulders of stevedores . . .

HELLO MEMBERS OF THE ACADEMIA

What could they have known? The Atlantic, at the glass, taps

like an urchin cadging a sip of draft. Perhaps
each could count the glittering fish slipping the nets,

the dimes slipping from thread-worn pockets
leaving a shimmering trail leading to the stunted homes

of the poor, whose doors stutter in the storms that come
when the stove coughs its last and the kettle goes cold . . .

HELLO MEMBERS OF THE ACADEMIA

sky: black. now   mother's blankets
                are warm milk.
I remember   being a ghost.
                On Hallowe'ens,
in costume,   my face, a secret.
                My fall
blanching   into frost.
                Just a few
pages until   the green . . .

HELLO MEMBERS OF THE ACADEM{CUT TO DISNEY'S
THE JUNGLE BOOK:
an orangutan emerges from his study refreshed and a-singin}

20.
in cartoons, poisons always wear warnings of skulls & bones.
the rotgut jug? its Xs like 12 cars colliding in 3 intersections.

the black bomb wears a nametag. so does the white paint overflowing its can.
what is the warning in a black man in blackface?

who holds the bomb to read its name?
who ponders the danger of white paint?

21.
consider a hand puppet at the lectern. arms:
pinky and thumb of a party clown.

legs? nope, a wrist.
its voice pressed from stiff, red lips

as if from behind a brick wall.

question: what must a puppet feel like?
no, not yet. first, the backdrop:

the world is magic markered
to paper propped up

behind. the black magic
marker nearly dry from drawing

cosmoses, scenery.
one mustn't waste color, but

darkness must be total
(editing out light) yet

the magic marks go ragged
and sparse. the paper cosmos isn't black

but dirty and cloudy as a minstrel's hair.
what sort of universe is this? out of ink,

the red lips finally
fall open like a gallows trap.

voice escapes. the mouth
gulps the puppet: thumb, pinky, wrist.

the clown is a viper tasting its own tail.
this is my muse.

22.

question: what must a puppet feel like?

> *answer for a felt puppet*: spun cotton loose on the wind.
> *answer for a marionette*: dried fruit still on the limb.
> *answer for a paper bag puppet made in Sunday school*: I feel fine.

Amen.

23.

a man with a cell phone.
a man with a missing finger.
a man with a swinging golf club.
         how thirsty the ocean is,
         always clawing at the sand like
a man in a cartoon desert,
         clutching a bomb
         and drinking white paint for milk.
   ah, men and women bent and curved like alphabets.

like worms dodging pecking black birds.
like ballast tossed to the tides
from a Carolina-bound schooner.

24.

what of the Carolina dock?
deconstructed for lumber, made fine whalers of it. what do you make
of it? let's say: nothing.　　　　here,

take Dominguez's bourbon. remember
Dominguez? he lost his—nevermind—
take Dominguez's bourbon

splash it on the mast, the planks, the hull
take the cork (a smol-
dering blossom) let it drop. let it whisper to the liquor.

let the fire crawl over
everything like tourists. the wood blackens
up, this is the truth, you see? the smoke streaks the moon

as sooty fingers, the seagulls go dark as a pigeon
behind a check cashing joint,
the sheets are drying on November 1st

groped by ashes. the smirched birds
take the sky, cosmic paper in a gale, this is the truth, nahmean?

o ocean,
so hungry, and a bonfire, macaw-red. smoky
midnight hanging, black

call the poet "ocean."
what must one hunger for:

the pitch, the oysters, the pie
. . . sometimes the truth.

this is the poem
that will, that will

certainly, but
god-like? a ghost

among cattle? a viper
swallowing itself again

is the truth. you see
blackface, nahmean?

what is the warning?
hello members

of the Academia.
what could they have known?

what do you cook?
what do you hang?

what must it feel like?
what does this testify?

speak of fire, the first kiss
of flame to cork:

the cork is words.
I'll use my skin for paper.

26.

and the Man say:
"one day, this will all be yours":

chain link, flame shells, 40 bottle, party flyer, french fry, caution, black-
top, classifieds, rubber wrapper, catsup packet, fashion nails, sneaker sole,
jacket lining, paper cup, 2 for 1, dog shit, Mombo Wings, Lotto here, change-
purse, soda can, pickle stem, Funyun bag, Newport butt, discount gear, W-2,
bootleg tapes, razor wire, Wonder Bread, Bible study, oil puddle, Yaki braid: blonde

*   *   *   *

the sun lives in an abandoned Cadillac, and waits for Apollo to return
with gas money. she been waiting for years, and won't burn
without his lips behind her neck, at the roots where the peroxide
fries her blonde. he likes her better that way. besides
why not be yellow?

*   *   *   *

the schooners have learned to look like tenements. climb a fire escape,
the city spreads out before you, a dirty diorama at a suburban garage sale.

Muse in her sour t-shirt and bloody skirt. *while you're up there,*
look for some high yellow nigger. tell him

his baby mama gonna die in a busted Seville. tell him
bring his ass on home. about to be snowing out, bodies make heat.

27.

if the ink didn't dry, words could slip off the page like penguins
diving after smelt, and ravenous,
dragging themselves back onto an ice floe, gathering together for warmth,

(this is a metaphor for a sentence
broken down, you see that words alone are cold. that is enough for now.)

~~I could slip from the academic like penguins if the ink didn't dry~~
~~I could slip from the academic, penguin-like, but for the drying ink~~

nevermind—   ... that is enough for now.)

and the ice floe? I am an old man, riding it like a Cadillac into dusk.
one must be alone for such things and I have left my parka,
but I still smell of buffalo bull.

if this were a movie, old parka-less men would be melted out of ice floes.
they would collapse, first, like loosed marionettes. then, rise
to work their ancient northern magics against atomic milk and torpedos.

but this is a poem, so I leap from the ice floe, a tern
flying west, crying over Siberia's frostbitten cells
where the inmates die black from all the whiteness
and I perch here for a moment.

if this were a movie, we'd crosscut to the first African bleeding
at European feet, and while the blood ruins the pale sand,
the Europeans decide what to call the body so it isn't murder.

but this is a poem, nahmean? and it's easier to see
the tern making tern noises at a gangrenous prisoner
alone in an ice floe that won't move any closer to the sun

(this is a metaphor for a sentence ...
broken down, you see ...

~~I~~...
~~I~~...

nevermind

NOTES

AT THE PINK TEACUP
This poem references "The Cage" basketball court, located near the Village.

FAMILY ROOM
The film was *El Mariachi*, written and directed by Robert Rodriguez.

"LIVE/EVIL"
Pearl Cleage's complete quote reads: ". . . Miles was guilty of self-confessed violent crimes against women such that we ought to break his records, burn his tapes and scratch up his CDs until he acknowledges and apologizes and rethinks his position on the Woman Question." It appears in "Mad At Miles," an essay.

The Terrance Hayes quote is from "When the Neighbors Fight."

The Amaud Jamaul Johnson quote is from a phone conversation.

Miles Davis was married to Cicely Tyson.

POEM WITH SOME SAND AND ALL AT ONCE—SHAITAN
"Shaitan!/Sam'!/. . . Harmattan!/Sim'!/Kham'!" are, according to Roget, synonyms (some contracted) for sandstorms. There are darker meanings as well.

ANTHEM (COLLAPSING)
The Yusef Komunyakaa quote is from "Fever."

GRATITUDE (A HOPELESSLY INCOMPLETE LIST)

I must first thank my immediate family, Furman, Marcia and Dallas Kearney for teaching me to choose words first, but to always have something else "in case of weather."

Next, I must thank my kinfolk: the Kearneys, the Martins, the Buckleys, the Larkins, the Eptons, the Flukers, the Whites, the McConnells, the McJamersons, the Butlers, the Hearns, the Spears, the Swerdloffs and the Massalays.

Thanks to my writing peers, especially Kemp Powers, Jahsun, D. Zenani Mzube, Angela Boyce (RIP), Bao Phi, Nazirah, Toki, Yolanda Wisher, Eisa Davis, Tracie Morris, Reginald Harris, Jericho Brown, Brizzle, Abigail Garner, Dave Tomlinson, Jose Alvergue, Amar Rava, Vejea Jennings, Jen Hofer, Maria Dahvana Headley, Terrance Hayes, my San Diego posse, my Twin Cities folk, the CC massive, CalArts MFA peeps and the 2004 Bread Loaf Waiters.

My teachers, especially, Mrs. Ivory, Mrs. Toh, Dr. Frost, Dr. Washington, Dr. Redd, dj Watson, Cornelius Eady, Toi Derricotte, Harryette Mullen, Tim Seibles, Nikky Finney, Al Young, Michael Harper, Elizabeth Alexander, Marilyn Nelson, Hermine Pinson, Christine Wertheim, Janet Sarbanes, Jon Wagner, Matias Viegener, Dodie Bellamy, Forrest Hamer, Carl Phillips, Natasha Trethewey, Li-Young Lee, Dr. Charles H. Rowell and Dr. Jo Berryman.

Special thanks to Angela Jackson for believing in me enough to call me a poet and to David St. John for believing in me enough to refer me to Red Hen Press.

Thanks Kate and Mark, for falling asleep at the switch and letting me through.

To Alameda Street, Altadena, HAGLC, John Muir High School, Howard University, Writerzblock, Cave Canem (especially to Carolyn Micklem), California Institute of the Arts, Callaloo Creative Writer's Workshop and Uncle Sam for providing the environments necessary to develop my voice.

Yona Harvey, Amaud Jamaul Johnson and Tracy K. Smith for their generosity and rigor in helping me tweak this manuscript. If you see something wack in here, it's probably because I was too hard headed to listen to them.

Like all the gangsta rappers say at award shows: "I thank God."

And to Nicole, for her patience and love, support, good sense and good ear.

You each deserve so much more than a simple thank you.

Printed in the USA
CPSIA information can be obtained
at www.ICGtesting.com
JSHW051916150424
61217JS00006B/305